Illusion:

My Journey Into Reality

By Melanie Thiede

Order this book online at www.trafford.com
or email orders@trafford.com

Most Trafford titles are also available at major online book retailers.

Printed in Victoria, BC, Canada.

ISBN: 978-1-4269-2689-1

*Our mission is to efficiently provide the world's finest, most comprehensive book publishing
service, enabling every author to experience success. To find out how to publish your book, your
way, and have it available worldwide, visit us online at www.trafford.com*

Trafford rev. 4/12/2010

 www.trafford.com

North America & international
toll-free: 1 888 232 4444 (USA & Canada)
phone: 250 383 6864 ♦ fax: 812 355 4082

Table of Contents

Le Petit Printemps

Le petit printemps

Tout vert, tout vert

Remplace l'hiver

Tout blanc, tout blanc

C'est une moineau

Tout gris, tout gris

Qui me l'a dit?

Qui me l'a dit?

Spring 1987

What Makes Me Smile?

What makes me happy

When I ride my bike outside

When I meet and greet last years teachers

When mom makes her chop suey.

November 1987

Remembrance Day

Remembering the dead

Embrace someone you love

Mourning, what you do after someone dies

Empty your life is when they die

Mornings you're alone

Bidding good-bye!

Rose which we place on the grave

Angry after they die

Nourishment neglected

Caring for loved ones

Exactly the end of this

Dove means peace

Above in Heaven

Yesterday I was okay.

Spring 1988

Giving Thanks

I thank thee for the

Trees and the breeze

For the flea and the bee

I thank thee.

For the buds that bloom

For the bed and the broom

Also for the bear and the air

I thank thee.

We dine while sipping wine

Tonight under the stars

Not in the car or in our home

I love thee. I thank thee.

September 1990

My Opinions

I like school

I like soccer

I love myself

I'm Me.

Me and Mom

Me and Dad

I don't care

I love both

I'm Me.

Old or young

Your parents may be

They're still yours

I'm Me.

September 1990

Growing Up

I used to crawl

I felt like I had to bawl

Now I walk and talk

Speaking in half rhymes

Now uttering in rhyme no more.

November 1990

Work

When you work

Scrubbing floors, doors

Windows too- it all

Seems to be the same.

Scrub the shelves down

Tables need to squeak as they

Are cleaned- time to

Recycle the towels I used

Outside the birds sing.

September 1991

The Planets & Our Sun

All I need are the planets

Mars, Jupiter, and Mercury

All I need are my friends

Wherever they may be

They are important to me.

Influenced by the sun for growth

Decisions made easier by numbers

Emotions to guide me to the north star

Friendships cultivated with the Earth

They are all important to me.

With the moons swinging by

Picking up the colors of the sea

Alternating control with the sun

Cultivating, growing with each

Passing year and day

They are important to me.

September 1991 (completed December 2008)

friends

Friends can help you

Friends can talk to you

They laugh with you, not at you

They play with you

They are just like me

Friends can read your mind.

September 1991
(Written in Conjunction
    with J. McNamara)

What is Love?

Love, Love

It's everywhere

But what is love?

Love, care and adore

You can love a partner

You can care for a toy

I like when adore

Is around to play

Love is a heart

That never goes away

If love isn't there

You have not been alive.

Spring 1992

Life Isn't fair

You can't always get

Everything that you want

If you have to leave

You've got to do it

Leaving your friends

A half an hour away

Living where you don't do anything

Except watch the television set

When you want to play

You have to telephone

Decide where you want to go

Drive for a while in your vehicle

But life isn't fair

When kids are mean

You can either fight or leave.

Fall 1992

Love Is Great

Love is great,

If you have one love in your life

You will be happy; know you are lucky

If your love leaves you

You will miss them; it is okay to cry

You can always find another

There are wonderful people everywhere.

Fall 1992

L'Amour Est Magnifique

L'Amour est magnifique

Si tu as une amoureux dans at vie

Ta vie aurais bonne la restant de at vie

Si ton amoureux te laisse

Tu vas etre triste, tu peut trouver une autre.

Fall 1992

What Is A Cloud?

A cloud is a thing

That gives us rain

Which makes flowers grow

A cloud brings chills

A cloud bring the breeze

I don't know how

The clouds do all of these

We need the clouds

Rain and thunder maybe not

Leave some time for the sun.

Fall 1992

friendship

You're especially nice to be around

And you're my friend

I'm so happy I've got a pal

To tell my feelings to

No one else means more to me than you.

Spring 1992

Love Is Great Revisited

Love is great

If you have one love in your life

You'll be happy

However if your lover leaves you

You'll miss them greatly

There may be another person waiting for your love

Just around the corner- go find them!

Fall 1992

My Love

My love went away and

May never come back

I cried many nights

I'll miss her

My love left me

Or did I leave her?

She's gone far away

May never come back.

May 1993

War 2

War, who likes war?

War is fighting and death

It can change your life.

If a loved one dies you will cry

You'll mourn for them, you may live on.

A Sister's Love Survives

What is a sister? you ask

I think I may know but I'm not sure

What is a friend? You ask again

A friend stands by you in all cases, scenarios

How do you know you have a true friend? You observe.

You shape your own life according to your views

Borrow views and opinions of others

Or create your own version with a mixed view

A sister's love can survive the biggest fights

Can survive throughout world wars

Will always exist, no matter what

As we care connected on a spiritual level

We have become inseparable, through time and space

We were always one, and will always be.

I was unsure I would succeed

You stood by me and encouraged me

Little by little I grew

We helped each other past our fears

Grew closer throughout the years.

This is what a sister's love is all about

A Sister's Love Survives.

November 1993

Bicycles

Bicycling

Speeding, slowing

Stop, look, going

Think, crossover look, speed up

Car, slowly, faster

Trying, failed- dead.
Spring 1993

Pearls

Pearls are bright

Bright, sunlight

Dive, search, seashells

Catch, open, dead, disappointed

Bring and return to air.

Spring 1993

When I Was Five

Standing in the snow

Eulogy being given by a minister

Family crying all around me

While granddad was interred.

This all happened when I was five.

I stood there frozen and unsure

As rules hadn't been explained

Mother was now fatherless

Grandmother was a widow

They loved him very much

People watched and cried

Standing around a grave

When I was five.

Mom was trembling

How could I help as I was only five?

I went to hold mother, to show I cared.

It was okay to miss him.

All this happened when I was five.

January 1994

My Child's Word

I've traveled far- to many of life's destinations
Looking for answers to all of life's questions
I was amazed at how few I found
I looked in some of the corners of our world
Other people were asking the same questions
And had not found the answers.
When I finally got home
I found that my life was nearly over and not

One of my questions had been answered
When I was on my deathbed
My child told me the answer to my one and only question;

Had I helped anyone? - Had I made a difference?
Her answer was the last thing I heard

- Yes.

January 1994

Memories

Lying on the sand

On a deserted beach

Thinking of the past

Remembering the times I spent there

When I was young.

Building sand castles and playing in the sand.

What great memories!

Spring 1994

Ice Cream Sundae

Here I have a huge cup

Filled with ice cream and other goodies

Strawberry, Chocolate, Vanilla

Yum, Yum, Yum.

First I eat the cherry

Second I eat the whipping cream

Third I eat the sprinkles

Rich, Rich, Rich.

Second to last I eat the chocolate syrup

Fifth I eat what I've been waiting for

I start with the Vanilla, then Chocolate

Wow, Wow, Wow.

There's only one thing left

I eat the Strawberry ice cream

I lick up the rest

It's gone, gone, gone.

Spring 1994

Consequences

For every action

There is a reaction

That is a constant

So is learning a constant.

By cheating on something

You only cheat yourself

Not others but only you

I have learned the hard way.

Some advice for students and youth

Always be honest in everything you do

You will succeed even if it takes a little more time

You will go far.

If you cheat yourself it will be with you

For a very long time

You will never forget it.

December 1995

Goodnight, Dear One

We were frolicking through

The flowers; we were beloved

You made my life richer

With your caring ways

You saved my life over and over

I owe you a heavenly lot

We parted and stayed silent

Not even saying goodbye.

Now I find you again and wonder

Can we turn on our emotions

Like an old fashioned light switch?

Our time together is and always will be priceless to me.

Spring 1995

Memories With her

Days were spent in the Jalara jungle

Lovers curling up together like spoons

Never were they intertwined

Like the two twin moons

Turning around each other

While glistening from the heat

Only saying what needed to be said.

Spring 1995

The World 2

In the world there are animals

They come in all sizes

There's one common thing

They are all earthlings.

Some have different ways of traveling

Others have different markings

They all have their own unique voice

They have many colors.

In the world there are plants

There are those with flowers

That feel wet with the morning dew

Others stay dry to the touch

There are so many species

Plants, birds and reptiles alike

That may go unnoticed or

Undiscovered.

Let us discover the things

That have not been explored

We belong to the planet

That we know so little about

All life forms are unique

They all have faults too

Try to live in harmony

Get along with our comrades on this earth

Keep our planet clean

Our progeny will have a place

To call home that is livable; where the air is fresh

A clean and beautiful land to call home.

Spring 1996

You're Invisible To Me

You're invisible to me

I cannot say why

You are up north

And yet you are

Right near me

We walked along

The same muddy path

Somewhere you slipped

I paused and looked back

Saw nothing and continued

You're invisible to me

Yet you're right here with me.

Spring 1996

Inside Looking Out

An inclined roof extends from

My window like the peak of a waterslide

Opening the window, birds chirp outside

Dew dropped leaves and smells of chimney smoke

Grabbing a handful of raindrops

Cool, slippery and translucent raindrops

Realizing time is passing me by

The present is zooming by like cars on our street

The past wont come again

The future is starting now.

Fall 1996

Commuter Train

Pushing and shoving

Students everywhere in uniforms

Packed train, very little air

People eating oranges and chips

Next stop- who knows?

Little towns, Sweetness

Guys sharing a cigarette outside

Trains.

Fall 1997

Differences

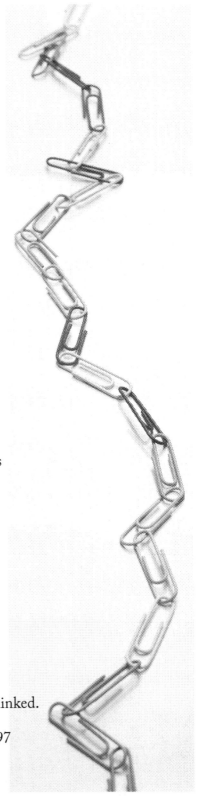

Though the difference is greater

Than we both expected

We ignored all others

Fighting for love against ideals

We thought distance would be all

That which would cure set ideals

For we now know

That distance doesn't matter much

For we are connected at our core

The direct center of our being

Connected , our bodies with each others

Emotions are not linear

Nor are they logical

Distance is not related

Emotions will shine through

We are apart but still

We are connected like rubber cement

Cemented at our hearts and our minds linked.

November 1997

Picture by: Anonymous

Disabling Attacker

Why must it always be me?

Whom you latch on to and put down?

If a fly flew by, would you tear off

It's wing, disabling it?

If a herd of zebra ran through your territory

Would you paint the stripes

A different color, red perhaps?

Why must it always be

The lesser and smaller

People you attack

The weak against the strong

Two animals of the same

Species confront at a lake

One of them knows how to swim,

The other does not–

Why does it have to be me?

March 1997

My Healer

Now I am healed - running into the water

Finding Aphrodite waiting - waiting just for me.

My journey, skipping - through the fields

Fields of strawberries

Berries for my enjoyment.

Jumping through the silver zero

Into a land full of joy and love

Following my internal directions

Through the whole in the zero.

Hopping through the wrought iron gates

To the city in gold beyond

Filled with gold and bronze

Healing me with light.

Coming back to reality slowly

Delaying, swimming with Aphrodite

Smiling with complete

Complete familiar surroundings.

Now I am healed - my Opa is my healer

In the skin of a dolphin

Healing me, loving me.

Fall 1997

Linked Destiny

It was meant to be this way for a reason

They say that love is blind and lovers blinded

Were we blind to love? Or to the world?

Were we just not looking close enough?

True love is capable of lasting seconds or

Even multiple lifetimes

For time is irrelevant - man made

We can make it through time and distance

Making it fly by, fly higher than the eagles

Run like a greyhound or

Swim and jump like dolphins in the sea

If it was meant to be we will know

By each other's heart

For we are connected at the center

Connected at our heart

For forever is never-ending.

October 1997

The Loneliest Place

I am sitting here on what seems to me

To be the loneliest place there is

I am here however- watching people go by

Here I go and here I stay

I am sitting on a rock and a hard place

This place is here forever

However I will not be here as long

As this solid stone is smooth from seawater

Flowing over it day by day

By night this is here always

Sitting here waiting for something to happen

So shall I stay until it does?

November 1997

Paper Clip Love

You filled my world with love

Emptied the unkindness and despair

Out of my being-

Filling me with joy and happiness

The joy brought back from

The long sojourn someplace else

Love and peace now return to my soul

For which I am eternally grateful

Intermittently sending you a percentage

Of the greatest love, peace and joy

That I had forgotten that I had

And had shoved aside

While flowers and trees die

My love for you will never end

For we are attached at the center

Like paper clips in a linked row.

November 1997

Les Flocons De Neiges

Le temps qu'on a passé ensemble

Est comme des flocons de neiges

En tombant d'une arbre

Chaque une est differente

Flocons se passent en avant de nos yeux

Les yeux bleues, et bleues-gris

Les yeux ouverts en regardent

Les flocons et les feuilles qui tombent

D' arbustres qu'on a poussé d'une graine

On les voies toutes

C'est exceptionnelle la façon que

Deux personnes qui sont si differentes

Mais en-dessous on est si semblable

Peuvent reacter comme s'est passé

Les coeurs ont été libèré de leurs cages

Les coeurs s'ouvrent sans jugement, sans opinions

Pour moi ça signifie un destin qui á nous presenter.

December 1997

Les Nuits Sans Coeur

Les nuits qui s'en viennent serront

Les plus difficiles mais

On va les gagner - notre amitie

Avec aucun vagues a sursauter

Les jours que je m'ennuie

Au milieu de ça, je pense á vous

Des pensées que je ne veut pas oublir

Les nuits sans coeur

C'est les nuits que vous n'êtes pas là

A côté de moi en me parlant

Des choses qui se passent

Les nuits sans vous sont

Des nuits sans coeur.

December 1997

It Was Meant To Be

It was meant to be

I feel it in my soul, in my bones

True love is capable of

Lasting decades or only seconds

For time is IRRELEVANT, man made

We can make it through time and distance

We will surely see

If it was meant to be

The quality and amount of our contact

Will tell if this is true

Even though we are linked together

Linked at the center

Words can clutter or they can clarify

Expressing words and feelings

Over great distances

Still we are linked with our hearts.

Are you game? I certainly am.

December 1997

The Universe and Me

I have changed much since the moving of the planets

New axis and new air moving people around

Rules and processes changing every day

Practicing how to be me every day.

Hiding forever dodging social events

Used to be me in years gone by.

Those social events, the making of friends

Introducing myself to others

Had to be learned by me as fear came trembling down

My spine and my breath quickened pulse increased

Speeches would need to be done, I could do them

Still the fear held me captive most of the time

Held hostage by inhibitions and past experiences

Yet set free by the occasional encouragement

My will was not strong then

To succeed, to speak out, to cheer others on when I might.

Living with people who have patience, knowing that

They took the time to listen and hear what I really was about

Helping me at every turn, steering me in the right direction

I will succeed now, thanks to those who listened and heard the real me.

Fall 1998

Distance

I wish with all my heart

Upon a shining star

You were here

Here with me

Hearing your voice

So sweet and caring

Yet so far away

Far from my reach

I yearn to hold your hands

To have you near

Just to be with you

The distance between us

I hold you dear in my heart

Now and forever, I promise

I'll be with you someday

I'll be by your side someday

Someday soon.

October 1998

from Me to You

A word when you're lonely

A guide when you're searching

Someone who shares your laughter

Someone who shares your tears

Someone who understands you

Someone whom you need in difficulties

Someone who knows your tears

Someone you love to be with

Someone who makes you smile

Will never be out of style

That's what a special friend is

And here's how you know it's true

Because I am a friend of yours.

October 1998

Conflicts

Conflicts resolve people into acting

Changing something, somehow

People cannot resolve something in themselves

Only time, caring and support can cure these.

February 1999

High and Low

At a time in my life

Feeling low and grayish

Searching for my river

My path to follow- to dream

Of successes to come

My path has been mucky

Soiled with puddles

Ankle deep in water

Trying to escape

Reading books helped me through

At one point in my life

Lows and highs succeeded each other

Quickly like a hummingbird in flight

Above a succulent flower.

April 1999

The Real Me

If you see me walking down the street

Stop and say hello if my head hangs low

If I appear to be happy look again

For deep inside may be anger or fear

Inside you may see something

You may see the real me.

You stop and ask me why

I am humming a war song

I reply that I do not know

In my most deep thoughts

You will find all answers

The Real Me.

In my life I wear many masks

Some of which aren't clear

Others are definitely transparent

They show the world the Real Me.

Get to know me, calm me down

Make me feel at ease, I will respond

Take off the masks one by one

I may let you see the Real Me.

April 1999

Lonely In Thought

Lonely as I have ever been

Feeling this way as I am here

Empty because I am without

My littlest angel

School is going all right

Success will come my way

Time is all I need and discipline

By myself and me, my lord and my friend

The angels above me - hovering at the ready to assist

I am calling to those who care

To help me, please!

For I know that I need-

Someone to watch over me.

May 1999

Ce Que Je Vois

Les rues autours de moi

Le vent au toit

Arbustre sur droite

Une chaîne sur la gauche

Pour moi je les voies

Les toits vert, rouge et gris

Les lumières au coin

Je vois les oiseaux

L'eau viens de la piscine

S'en va par les trous de la piscine

En les regardent je vois

Ce qu'ils veulent

La porte s'ouvre et ils s'en vont

Je regarde les arbres

Le vent autour de moi

Les rues s'enferment

Comme une boite autour de moi.

October 1999

My Family, My Home

Reuniting, becoming clearer, calmer

Family coming together again

Coming into my heart from far away

Friends are family too at my core

My home is being filled with family

With joyous love and wisdom

Members and friends that had been forgotten

My home and my family together again as a whole.

Generations gone by taught their young

To fly away early and find a mate

Who would bring prosperity and wealth

As well as offspring to the family to keep their lineage going

People missed the point, most of the time and marriages were moot

Youth in my generation believe that it is a choice

To love, care for and marry a person regardless of gender or sex

To work or serve a spouse, to help others and to love one another

There is growth in this realization and wisdom too.

March 2000

Peace & War

Peacefully sitting in class

Listening to tanks

Filled with people who want to help

Our country under attack

The younger children were fearful

The others cheered them up

Telling them that it will be okay

While bombshells are flying

Just overhead.

September 2001

Explorer

Out of the darkness- I heard a shout

You came from around the tree

And smiled at me

Bright and wise; smart and deep

The light through which my candle shines

Though our time on this spinning globe is short

Our paths crossed and so began our journey

Whether be short or lasting

Am sure that we will see

The beauty that was meant to be.

Spring 2001

Alone on a Special Day

There came a time when

I could have left you

Without telling you

Just how much I care

There are no words to express it

I would have died for you

Instead, you died for me

I guess that shows just how much

You cared for me

You stood in line like you should have

Then you took a stand, and lost your life

Now you've gone and left me

It's my first year without you

On this Special Day

I wish I could say, "happy valentine's day!"

Winter 2001

What Children Mean To Me

Children are our legacy

They show us right from wrong

Through the things they do

They have an ability to cheer us up-

When no one else can-

They are our kids.

They allow us to be vulnerable sometimes

Kids do not judge us by our appearances

Kids show us how to be heroes

Children have courage and wisdom

That sometimes is uncanny.

You see things in them that you

May not like in yourself

Others that you can't explain-

Kids are like mirrors and textbooks

You learn every step of the way.

Legacies left - History passed on and on

Family created and molded;

To be loved and to love in return

This is what children are;

Children are love and lifelong learning.

May 2003

Cherished friendships

Yesterday, my friend listened to what I had to say

Reassured me, telling me that it'll be okay

My beliefs were shaky, yet I accepted her reply

Hearing those words uttered with affection

Made all my worries fade away.

When my world was falling apart

Words of courage were spoken

Enough to make my fears go away

Supporting me in the trials of life and love

Yesterday, my friend was there.

Reconnecting with ones you love

Speaking as though time had stood still

Reaching out, smiling, knowing

Letting me know again it'll be okay

Today, my friend is back again.

Worlds apart with hearts aglow - connected

Friendships never seemed so harmonious

Waiting for an old message in a bottle

That was tossed in the ocean

Dear One, Will you be there tomorrow?

September 2008

Journey Through Time

Throughout my years on this Earthly plane

This one and only Earthly plane

I have known deep down that I had

A soul mate out there somewhere

Question was would I find her?

After years of searching

Exploring this Earthly plane

My spirit had been shattered to its core

By prior experiences and attackers

Whom I thought I loved- had hurt me

How much longer do I have to wait?

Nearing the point of giving up

That is when I found her!

Where? Right where she had been all along

Right under my nose! So to speak, of course...

However the timing was not quite right

How long would I have to wait?

With eyes vibrant with life's sparkle

A door opened just beyond

The window to her soul - our connection grew

Intensified- waiting for her to be mine once again.

January 2009

Feelings From Forever

I was feeling all this love

So I wrote her a poem

Professing my love for this lady

Promising her my undying love

Knowing nothing could become if it

Nothing until later

The feeling came out of forever

Finding me and her together

Only for a second did I hear

Her love for me, that was there

It was there.

Seeing her bow shaped smile

Topaz colored eyes smiling at me daily

Aglow with life and love each day

I caught many of her glances

I always replied.

My love for her has remained un-tattered

It has evolved but has remained pure

Everlasting, sensual and true in nature

Her lilting sweet voice rings in my ears

Thinking about her holding me close

Rocking back and forth, cuddling up

Years later this could come to fruition.

My heart beats faster, my blue eyes aglow with hope

Still recalling her footsteps, the sound of her walking

Down the halls and into the room each day

Longing for her touch and to hear her voice once again

Makes my heart and soul tingle thinking of her

My love for her has remained as strong and has evolved

She reacted with shock and fear; did not directly speak

I know that her love for me has remained; I await her reply

My love, will you speak with me again?

February 8, 2009